UNDERTAKER
LIFE OF THE DEAD MAN

by Pamela Dell

Consultant:
Mike Johnson, Writer
PWInsider.com

CAPSTONE PRESS
a capstone imprint

Velocity is published by Capstone Press,
1710 Roe Crest Drive, North Mankato, Minnesota 56003.
www.capstonepub.com

Library of Congress Cataloging-in-Publication Data
Dell, Pamela.
    Undertaker : life of the dead man / by Pamela Dell.
    p. cm. — (Pro wrestling stars)
    Includes bibliographical references and index.
    Summary: "Describes the life of Undertaker, both in and out of the ring"—Provided by
publisher.
    ISBN 978-1-4296-8679-2 (library binding)
    ISBN 978-1-62065-363-0 (ebook pdf)
    1. Undertaker, 1965—Juvenile literature. 2. Wrestlers—United States—Biography—
Juvenile literature. I. Title.
GV1196.U54D45 2013
796.812092—dc23 [B]   2012011306

Editorial Credits

Mandy Robbins, editor; Sarah Bennett, set designer; Kyle Grenz, book designer;
    Laura Manthe, production specialist

Photo Credits

AP Images for Mattel: David Goldman, 45 (action figures); AP Images for WWE Corp.: Paul
Abell, 19; AP Images: Chris Carlson, 5 (middle); Corbis: Sygma/Uli Rose, 28; Dreamstime:
maximus, 19 (tv), 55hasan, 45 (DVDs), Andrea Degano, 23 (fireplace), Balazs Justin, 8
(tie), Baloncici, 38 (stretcher), Caranica Nicolae, 25 (hearse), Ctacik, 8 (cravat), Elswarro,
12-13, Eyewave, 22 (trash can), Hellem, 24 (urn), Iaroslav Neliubov, 38 (boxing ring),
Jaroslaw Grudzinski, 16-17 (background), Koya79, 7 (gravestone), 27 (gravestone), Marko
Bradic, 24 (casket), Mexrix, 22 (equipment), Neil Lockhart, 6 (inset), Nikita Buida, 5
(druids), Pennywise, 8 (spats), Scubabartek, 5 (Stonehenge), Win Nondakowit, 23 (ladder),
Yevgen Chornobay, 33 (background); Getty Images: LatinContent/Jam Media/Alfredo Lopez,
16 (right), LatinContent/Jam Media/Gerardo Zavala, 20-21, WireImage/Bob Levy, 26,
WireImage/KMazur, 17 (inset), WireImage/Tiffany Rose, 42; Globe Photos, 15, 39 (left), 41,
Globe Photos: John Barrett, 32, Kelly Dawes, 43; Landov: PA Photos/Simon Galloway, 33;
Newscom: Splash News/Heather Rousseau, 7 (right), 29, WENN Photos DM2, 9, ZUMA
Press, 5 (inset), 27, 30 (both), 31 (both), 37, cover, ZUMA Press/Globe Photos/John Barrett,
18 (bottom), ZUMA Press/Graham Whitby, 39 (right), ZUMA Press/UPN-TV/WWF, 16
(left), 18 (top); Nova Development Corporation, 44 (reels); Photo by Wrealano@aol.com,
13, 34-35; Shutterstock: Bruce Works, 25 (shovel), Danny E Hooks, 23 (chair), didden, 24
(hammer), Katrina Brown, 6-7 (background), Kirsty Pargeter, 14 (inset), mayawizard101, 33
(heart), Molodec, 37 (background), raresirimie, 39 (tacks), Shumadinac, 14 (inset), skvoor, 11
(Texas), VikaSuh, 11 (buildings); Wikimedia: Fatima, cover, 1 (background), Felipe Bascunan,
14, Mandy Coombes, 10, swiftwj, 24 (Kamala), Vishal Somaiya, 36

Artistic Effects

Dreamstime, Shutterstock

Printed in the United States of America in Stevens Point, Wisconsin.
032012   006678WZF12

TABLE OF CONTENTS

ENTER THE UNDERTAKER

"GONG! GONG!"

As the booming gong tolls, the arena goes dark except for eerie lights glowing through billowing smoke. Electric-blue bolts of electricity zap the air. Haunting funeral music plays. A thrill rushes through the crowd.

From the spooky gloom, a man emerges. Backlit, he creates a huge silhouette. He appears as a haunting figure from the Old West, with long dark hair and a long dark coat. A Stetson cowboy hat shades his face.

As the menacing presence slowly strides toward the wrestling ring, an announcer's voice blasts:

"Weighing 299 pounds ... the challenger from Death Valley ... The Undertaker!" The crowd erupts in cheers.

Undertaker's signature entrance style always creates a huge buzz. But the big payoff happens in the ring. Undertaker routinely bends, twists, and slams his opponents to the mat. Taking on "The Dead Man" is no easy task.

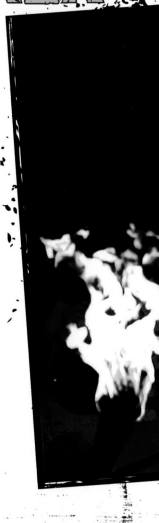

CHAPTER 1

GOT TO HAVE A GIMMICK

The idea of modeling a pro wrestling character after an undertaker, or **mortician**, from the Old West has turned out to be more of a hit than anyone could have imagined. Undertaker is a legendary favorite. He is big, bad, mean, and one of the greatest all-stars in pro wrestling.

FACT

Undertaker won *Wrestling Observer Newsletter's* Best Gimmick award for five years straight—from 1990 through 1994.

A GIMMICK THAT WORKS

Undertaker claims to have come from the dark side. A common slogan warns, "He buries them alive!" He's been billed as "The Dead Man from Death Valley." "Rest in Peace" is often his parting comment at the end of an interview.

All this is part of the Undertaker's **gimmick**, the unique image he's created as a pro wrestler. His undead **mortician** character was an immediate hit from the first time he used it in 1990. The gimmick has had undying appeal ever since.

gimmick—a clever trick or idea used to get people's attention

mortician—a person who prepares dead bodies for funerals

DRESSED TO KILL

FIRST LOOK

From the beginning, Undertaker made sure he was dressed to kill. When he first came on the scene, his signature apparel wasn't just a long trench coat and the Stetson. He also wore gloves, a button-down shirt, and a tie. Frequently he even wore **spats**, a kind of open-toe boot covering.

TRENCH COAT

Taker's trench coat is made of long, black leather that reaches below his knees.

Tie

Taker sometimes wore a conservative striped tie in his early days.

Tattoos

Taker's tattoos are legendary. His tattoos include skulls, messages on scrolls, and a bearded man. He also has a tattoo of a spooky-looking figure in a red-hooded robe on a throne topped with skulls.

Cravat

A cravat was another early option. This is an old-fashioned type of neckwear. It was popular before ties came along. Undertaker usually preferred purple cravats.

GLOVES

Undertaker has worn all kinds and colors of gloves—short, long, fingerless, black, blue, and gray.

THE STETSON

This cowboy hat was designed by John B. Stetson in the 1860s. It was nicknamed "The Boss of the Plains" hat. The Stetson is still a big seller.

TODAY'S LOOK

More recently, Undertaker's look has been trimmed back. A black tank top has replaced his shirt and tie. He rarely wears spats. But you might see him wearing nearly knee-high lace-up boots.

CHAPTER 2

WRESTLER ON THE RISE

Undertaker was born Mark Calaway on March 24, 1965. His pro wrestling career began in Texas in 1984. Before he tried his hand at pro wrestling, Mark was hoping for a career as a basketball player. He played basketball in high school and college but changed his course when he became interested in pro wrestling.

1984 Mark made his **debut** in the Texas-based World Class Championship Wrestling (WCCW).

1988 Mark joined the Continental Wrestling Association (CWA), based in Tennessee.

The young wrestler signed with World Class Championship Wrestling (WCCW), a regionally broadcast pro wrestling company in Texas. There he went by the name Texas Red. Over the next five years, Mark moved up the ranks. By 1989 he had joined World Championship Wrestling (WCW). This promotion company was nationally televised.

FACT

Mark had a big year in 1989. He won the United States Wrestling Association (USWA) Unified World Heavyweight Championship. He also won the World Championship Wrestling Association's (WCWA) Texas Heavyweight Championship.

At WCW, Mark changed his ring name to Mean Mark Callous. He became part of a **tag team** called the Skyscrapers. He teamed up first with Dan Spivey and then with a wrestler called the Masked Skyscraper. When the team broke up, Mark took up singles competitions.

1990 Mark joined the World Wrestling Federation (WWF), now known as World Wrestling Entertainment (WWE).

LatE 1989 Mark ended up in the newly created United States Wrestling Association (USWA), a merger between CWA and WCCW. Mark then joined World Championship Wrestling (WCW).

debut—a first public appearance

tag team—when two wrestlers partner together against other teams

FINAL RESTING PLACE

LAST LAUGHS

In 1990 the WCW decided not to renew Mean Mark Callous' contract. They seriously doubted he had what it took to become a big-time, crowd-pleasing winner. Years later, Undertaker explained it in an interview. "They told me I wouldn't amount to anything in this business. That people would never buy tickets to see me wrestle. They really censored me and told me I had no personality."

The decision was their loss. In 1990 Mark signed on with the World Wrestling Federation (WWF), the top-ranked pro wrestling company. November 22, 1990 was a landmark day in the WWF. It was the day Ted DiBiase Sr. introduced a new member to his Million Dollar Team at the 1990 SURVIVOR SERIES. DiBiase's highly anticipated mystery team member was called Cain the Undertaker.

SURVIVOR SERIES:
An event in which teams of wrestlers face off against each other in a series of intense matches. The last team standing wins!

This match marked the beginning of Undertaker's long, fascinating career with the WWF. With more than 20 years in the ring, he sets the record for the company's longest-active wrestler.

FACT

In 2002 the WWF changed its name to World Wrestling Entertainment to avoid a lawsuit. The letters "WWF" were already associated with another organization—the World Wildlife Fund.

CHAPTER 3
CHANGING IT UP

Undertaker has been through a lot of changes in his long career. These include name changes, wardrobe changes, and especially attitude changes. He's flipped more than once from **heel** to **babyface** and back again.

ABOUt FaCE

Under the right circumstances, any heel or babyface might flip to the other side. When a good guy crosses over, it's called a "face-heel turn." Similarly, when a bad guy goes good, he's said to have made a "heel-face turn," or "turned face."

Heels are not universally despised, however. Some of wrestling's biggest heels—like Undertaker—have been extremely popular with fans. In fact, when a babyface with a weak fan following suddenly turns heel, his audience appeal often skyrockets.

TAKER'S FIRST FLIP: FEBRUARY 1992

Undertaker turned from heel to face for the first time when he confronted Jake "The Snake" Roberts. Jake had been tormenting Miss Elizabeth, wrestler Randy Savage's wife and manager. This rubbed Undertaker the wrong way. When Undertaker confronted him, Jake demanded, "Whose side are you on?" The Undertaker growled, "Not yours!' With this remark, Undertaker became a babyface, taking the good side and winning the fans' admiration.

heel—a wrestler who acts as a villain in the ring

babyface—a wrestler who acts as a hero in the ring, often called a "face"

RETURN TO THE DARK SIDE

Playing a babyface wasn't a permanent condition for Undertaker. In the late 1990s he took a sharp turn back to the dark side, sending fans into a state of shock. Taker formed a **stable** called the Ministry of Darkness. It had the feeling of an evil **cult**.

The Ministry's stated aim was to unleash a "plague of evil" on WWE. Among other acts, the Undertaker kidnapped Stephanie McMahon, daughter of WWE owner Vince McMahon. He wanted to fulfill his dream of what he called their "black marriage." Stephanie was rescued by "Stone Cold" Steve Austin just in time.

stable—a group of wrestlers who protect each other during matches and sometimes wrestle together

cult—a strong, almost religious devotion to a person, a thing, an idea, or a way of life

THE MINISTRY OF DARKNESS CREW

The Ministry had many members who came and went. Undertaker's manager Paul Bearer was a founding member. Paul Bearer usually carried an **urn**, which supposedly gave Undertaker extra supernatural power. Other members of this stable of super-heels included wrestlers Faarooq, Bradshaw, Mideon, Viscera, and the Acolytes.

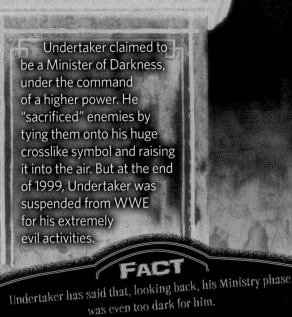

Undertaker claimed to be a Minister of Darkness, under the command of a higher power. He "sacrificed" enemies by tying them onto his huge crosslike symbol and raising it into the air. But at the end of 1999, Undertaker was suspended from WWE for his extremely evil activities.

FACT

Undertaker has said that, looking back, his Ministry phase was even too dark for him.

urn—a container made to hold the ashes of a cremated body

GET YOUR MOTOR RUNNIN'

Undertaker finally resurfaced in May 2000 at a WWE event called *Judgment Day*. He was sporting yet another new image. This time he showed up as a bad-boy biker. Undertaker made his entrances on a Harley-Davidson motorcycle. He still wore a trench coat, but he also wore jeans, sleeveless T-shirts, and bandannas. This new image became a big crowd-pleaser.

FACT

Every time Undertaker showed up in his biker image, he rode a different bike onto the scene. He borrowed them from local motorcycle dealers in the cities where his WWE events took place.

BACK TO BASICS

Undertaker rumbled through this biker version of his gimmick until the fall of 2002. Then he disappeared without a trace until mid-January 2003. Days before he came back, commercials were on TV promising "The Phenom" would return. Fans soon discovered that The Phenom was their old favorite, the Undertaker.

Taker returned with a vengeance. He showed up at the **ROYAL RUMBLE** on January 19th. Gone were all traces of the biker dude. No Minister of Darkness made an appearance. The Phenom came back as the true fan favorite—the original Undertaker. He has stayed the course ever since.

ROYAL RUMBLE

In this event, 30 wrestlers battle to be the last man standing. The match starts out with two wrestlers facing off. The other wrestlers enter at set times. The goal is to toss each opponent out of the ring. The last man left wins.

OCTOBER 1997

Bearer revealed a story about Undertaker's family dying in a fire—well almost all of his family. Taker's supposed brother, Kane, showed up to get his revenge.

MID-1997

After Undertaker won the WWF Championship, Bearer blackmailed the champ. He threatened to reveal a terrible secret of Taker's past unless he did everything Bearer ordered him to do. Undertaker refused.

APRIL 1998

Undertaker beat Kane by lighting his arm on fire.

MARCH 1998

Undertaker beat Kane at *WrestleMania* with Bearer's help.

EARLY 1999

Bearer had teamed up with Kane, but he deserted him to form the Ministry of Darkness with Taker.

FEBRUARY 1999

Undertaker beat Kane in a match by lighting his leg on fire.

Kane

Kane choke slammed Taker right through the ring floor.

A cement truck rolled in at the *Great American Bash*. After winning his match against the Dudley Boyz, Undertaker "buried" Paul Bearer in concrete.

Bearer turned on Undertaker during his match with Kane for the WWE World Heavyweight Championship. Taker lost when Bearer shone a light in his eyes to distract him.

— APRIL AND AUGUST 2001 —

Taker and Kane won the WWF Tag Team Championship both months.

— NOVEMBER 2006 —

Kane and Undertaker, the Brothers of Destruction, reunited after five years to defeat Mr. Kennedy and MVP three times in one night.

CHAPTER 4

BROTHERS OF DESTRUCTION

Who can you trust? If you're Undertaker, not his "brother" Kane! He's also been burned countless times by his manager, Paul Bearer. The tangled connections among these three have resulted in a maze of unpredictable moments.

CHAPTER 5

MONSTROUS MATCHES AND DEADLY MOVES

Pro wrestling has countless specialty matches. Some of WWE's most exciting gimmick matches originated with the Undertaker.

BOILER ROOM BRAWL (BRB)

Where does this match take place? Where else but in a boiler room. This part of a building contains the boiler, pipes, and lots of electrical equipment. The BRB match was born out of the rivalry between Undertaker and Mankind. Though not used much anymore, the BRB usually ends when one wrestler escapes the boiler room. Whoever gets out first wins the match.

BRB

FIRST USED
August 18, 1996

PLAYERS
Undertaker vs. Mankind

WINNER
Mankind

HIGHLIGHTS
Paul Bearer unexpectedly turned heel on Undertaker and slammed him over the head with his urn.

HELL IN A CELL

In a Hell in a Cell match, the entire ring and surrounding ringside are enclosed by a metal cage. This keeps wrestlers in and others out. These matches include weapons. Almost anything goes, even pipes, ladders, steel chairs, and more.

FACT

Undertaker competed in the first five Hell in a Cell matches and seven more after that. Of these matches, he has won five. Only Triple H has a better record. He has scored six wins.

HELL IN A CELL

FIRST USED
October 5, 1997

PLAYERS
Undertaker vs. Shawn Michaels

WINNER
Shawn Michaels (with Kane's help)

HIGHLIGHTS
Undertaker and Michaels fought for several minutes on top of the 20-foot (6-meter) cage before Undertaker flung his opponent off it.

There are only two ways to win a cell match: by submission or pin. If the opponent is down and taps the mat, he is signaling his submission. If this doesn't happen, the wrestler must pin his opponent to the mat, usually for a count of three.

Kamala was the first victim of a casket match.

CASKET MATCH

When the first Casket matches were held, the rules stated that the winner had to get his opponent into a ringside coffin and nail it shut. Things have eased up since then. For several years now, the only requirement has been that the coffin lid be securely closed.

CASKET MATCH

FIRST USED
November 24, 1992

PLAYERS
Undertaker vs. Kamala

WINNER
Undertaker

HIGHLIGHTS
Undertaker knocked Kamala out cold with Paul Bearer's mystical urn.

BURIED ALIVE MATCH

FIRST USED
October 20, 1996

PLAYERS
Undertaker vs. Mankind

WINNER
Undertaker

HIGHLIGHTS
Undertaker buried Mankind first, but then Mankind's pals attacked Undertaker. Mankind escaped and sent Undertaker to the grave. But WWF gave Undertaker the win.

BURIED ALIVE MATCH

These matches are so over-the-top that only a handful of them have ever been staged. An empty grave and a huge mound of dirt sit outside the ring. The object is to push the opponent out of the ring and bury him alive before the referee counts to 10.

LAST RIDE MATCH

In a Last Ride match, the rules are simple: there are none. To win, a wrestler has to do so much damage to his enemy that he's virtually senseless. The winner then has to stuff the loser into a **hearse** and drive it away.

LAST RIDE MATCH

FIRST USED
October 2, 2004

PLAYERS
Undertaker vs. John Bradshaw Layfield (JBL)

WINNER
JBL

HIGHLIGHTS
JBL smashed Taker in the face with a chair. Next, Jon Heidenreich showed up and smothered the Dead Man's face with a cloth soaked in something to make him pass out.

hearse—a car that carries a coffin to a funeral and burial

25

DEADLY
MOVES

Undertaker has plenty of power moves to smack down his opponents. But two of the best are the Chokeslam and his most famous finishing move, the Tombstone Piledriver. Here's how they're done.

CHOKESLAM

1. When the opponent approaches, Undertaker reaches out and grabs him tightly by the neck.

2. He places his other hand against his opponent's back.

3. Then Undertaker lifts his opponent up and holds him in the air for a frightening effect.

4. After that short pause, Undertaker slams him to the mat so he lands on his back.

TOMBSTONE PILEDRIVER

1. Undertaker grabs his opponent any way he can and turns him upside down, belly to belly.

2. Firmly grasping his opponent around the middle, Taker drops to his knees.

3. If his opponent is on his face when he collapses, Undertaker rolls him over onto his back.

4. Then Undertaker crosses his opponent's arms over his chest so he can "rest in peace."

CHAPTER 6

FEUDS AND BATTLE SCARS

When it comes to big, furious WWE **feuds**, Undertaker has had many. He's faced off with a long list of foes. Some rivalries stand out more than others.

Mankind wrestled wearing a mask. He took the mask off when he wrestled under his real name—Mick Foley.

MANKIND

HEIGHT
6 feet, 2 inches (188 cm)

WEIGHT
287 pounds (130 kilograms)

SIGNATURE MOVES
Mandible Claw; Double Arm DDT

UNDERTAKER VS. MANKIND

The year of 1996 included some especially beastly battles between Undertaker and Mankind. Their brawls raged well outside the ring, sometimes even into the fan-packed stands. One of their most memorable duels was at the first Boiler Room Brawl at *SummerSlam* in 1996. Undertaker's manager, Paul Bearer, betrayed him, helping Mankind take the victory.

STANDOUT MATCHES: UNDERTAKER VS. MANKIND

MATCH	WINNER
6-23-1996 **King of the Ring**	Mankind
8-18-1996 **Boiler Room Brawl**	Mankind
10-20-1996 **Buried Alive match**	Undertaker
11-17-1996 **Survivor Series**	Undertaker

feud—a long-running quarrel between two people or groups of people

UNDERTAKER VS. SHAWN MICHAELS

Shawn Michaels and Undertaker had fought together and against each other in tag teams since 1995. But it wasn't until 1997 that they came face-to-face in singles matches. That year Undertaker wrestled Michaels at *Bad Blood*, in the first ever Hell in a Cell match. From that point on, these two tangled in a long series of duels, with too many classic moments to count.

STANDOUT MATCHES: UNDERTAKER VS. SHAWN MICHAELS

MATCH	WINNER
10-5-1997 **First Hell in a Cell**	Shawn Michaels
1-18-1998 *Royal Rumble*	Shawn Michaels
1-28-2007 *Royal Rumble*	Undertaker
4-5-2009 *WrestleMania 25*	Undertaker
3-28-2010 *WrestleMania 26*	Undertaker

SHAWN MICHAELS

HEIGHT
6 ft, 1 in (185 cm)

WEIGHT
225 lbs (102 kg)

SIGNATURE MOVE
Sweet Chin Music

The feud with Michaels peaked with their brawls at *WrestleMania* 25 and 26. After Undertaker defeated Michaels at *WrestleMania 25*, Michaels bragged he was going to destroy Undertaker's *WrestleMania* winning streak at *WrestleMania 26*. Undertaker challenged Michaels to a "Streak versus Career" match. That meant if Michaels lost again, he'd have to permanently retire from pro wrestling. Michaels foolishly agreed. The match ended with a mighty Tombstone Piledriver, done by Undertaker. With that, Michaels' career was over. He has made very few appearances since that match.

UNDERTAKER VS. RANDY ORTON

Undertaker's feud with Randy Orton heated up in 2005. Orton had started calling himself the "Legend Killer." He claimed he could easily defeat longtime wrestling legends. Naturally, Undertaker was included on Orton's list of legends.

RANDY ORTON

HEIGHT
6 ft, 5 in (196 cm)

WEIGHT
235 lbs (107 kg)

SIGNATURE MOVE
RKO

STANDOUT MATCHES: UNDERTAKER VS. RANDY ORTON

MATCH	WINNER
4-3-2005 *WrestleMania 21*	Undertaker
8-21-2005 *SummerSlam*	Randy Orton
10-9-2005 *No Mercy*	Randy Orton & Cowboy Bob Orton
12-16-2005 *Smackdown!*	Randy Orton
12-14-2009 *Superstars of the Year*	Randy Orton

Throughout their rivalry, Orton bullied Undertaker. Sometimes he even got his father, Cowboy Bob Orton, to distract Undertaker during matches. These distractions helped the younger Orton defeat Undertaker several times. The Legend Killer planned to take Taker out for good at *WrestleMania 21*. He failed miserably, even with Cowboy Bob's help.

UNDERTAKER VS. BROCK LESNAR

The feud between Undertaker and Brock Lesnar flared during Undertaker's biker phase. The initial encounter happened backstage in September 2002, as so many of their brawls did. Lesnar and Undertaker were slated for a fight. Before the fight, Lesnar promised Undertaker's wife that he'd take care of her once he had demolished her husband.

BROCK LESNAR

HEIGHT
6 ft, 3 in (191 cm)

WEIGHT
265 lbs (120 kg)

SIGNATURE MOVES
F-5; Shooting Star Press First

In the ring at their 2002 *Unforgiven* match, Undertaker took revenge. He tossed Lesnar out of the ring several times. He also knocked out the referee. WWE officials thought he went a bit overboard. The match ended in a double disqualification.

STANDOUT MATCHES: UNDERTAKER VS. BROCK LESNAR

MATCH	WINNER
10-20-2002 *No Mercy*	Lesnar & Paul Heyman
8-28-2003 *Smackdown!*	Undertaker
10-19-2003 *No Mercy*	Lesnar & Vince McMahon
10-23-2003 *Smackdown!*	Undertaker

LOVE-HaTE RELAtiONSHiP?

Brock Lesnar became known for attacking Undertaker outside the ring. In the fall of 2003, within just a three-week period, Lesnar attacked Taker on multiple occasions backstage. Lesnar hit Undertaker with a steel chair. He smashed and bloodied Taker's head. And after a match on October 3, he broke Undertaker's hand with a steel tank. But even in the midst of this feud, the two men often wrestled as a team against other opponents.

BATTLE SCARS

So many battles over so many years adds up to a lot of physical damage. Every pro wrestler gets his or her share of battle scars. But despite the toll on his body, the Dead Man triumphantly rises to fight time and time again. Take a look at the body slams Taker has taken over the years.

FEBRUARY 2010

Undertaker suffered burns on his neck and chest after a fireworks display went wrong during his entrance into the arena. His coat went up in flames too.

JUNE 2010

Taker had surgery for yet another broken orbital bone after fighting Rey Mysterio. He also received a broken nose and a head injury in that match.

SUMMER 1995

Undertaker suffered a broken **orbital bone** after King Mabel did a leg drop on Taker's face.

NOVEMBER 2010
Undertaker seriously damaged his shoulder, requiring surgery.

NOVEMBER 2011
Taker had shoulder and hip surgeries to repair damage done over the years.

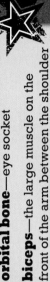

orbital bone—eye socket

biceps—the large muscle on the front of the arm between the shoulder and inner elbow

FEBRUARY 2000
Taker tore one of his pectoral, or chest, muscles.

OCTOBER 2002
Brock Lesnar smashed Undertaker with a propane tank, breaking the bones in Undertaker's right hand.

APRIL 2003
Undertaker had surgery on his left elbow after months of elbow problems and pain.

NOVEMBER 2006
Taker broke a rib during the WWE European tour.

JUNE 2007
Undertaker tore his left **biceps** muscle.

CHAPTER 7
IMMORTAL MOMENTS

Undertaker has supposedly returned from the dead more times than a cat with nine lives. He's been buried alive, sealed in coffins, set on fire, and hit by a car. Check out his most memorable death-defying moments.

JANUARY 22, 1994
ROYAL RUMBLE

Pro wrestler Yokozuna defeated Undertaker with the help of a handful of heels. They managed to stuff him into a coffin and began pushing it down the aisle. Lights began to flicker. A giant screen suddenly flashed the image of Undertaker's body. His voice rose as if from the grave, warning that he would not rest in peace.

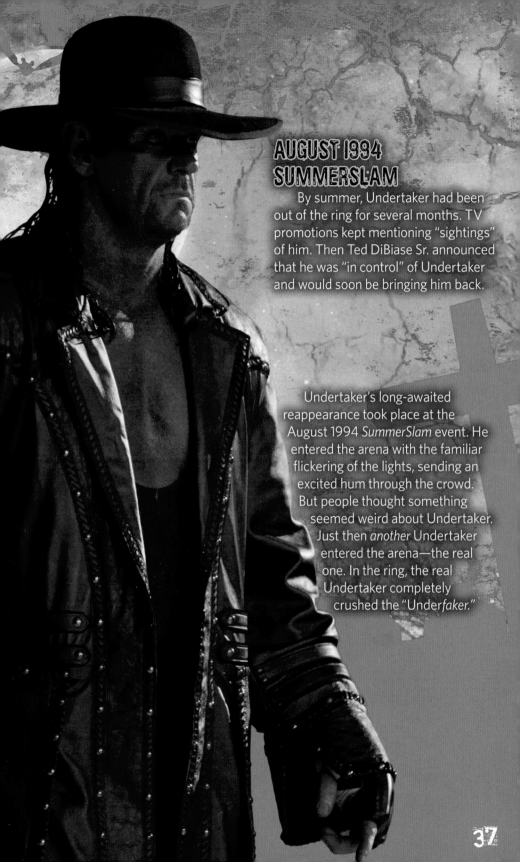

AUGUST 1994
SUMMERSLAM

By summer, Undertaker had been out of the ring for several months. TV promotions kept mentioning "sightings" of him. Then Ted DiBiase Sr. announced that he was "in control" of Undertaker and would soon be bringing him back.

Undertaker's long-awaited reappearance took place at the August 1994 *SummerSlam* event. He entered the arena with the familiar flickering of the lights, sending an excited hum through the crowd. But people thought something seemed weird about Undertaker. Just then *another* Undertaker entered the arena—the real one. In the ring, the real Undertaker completely crushed the "Under*faker*."

MOST MEMORABLE HELL IN A CELL

The 1998 *King of the Ring* match between Undertaker and Mankind tops the list of fans' favorite cell matches. At the time, fans had never seen a match as daring or graphic. Check out the play-by-play:

1 Mankind challenged Undertaker to start the match on top of the cage. Taker took the challenge and climbed the cell wall. After brawling with a steel chair, Undertaker threw Mankind off the top of the cage.

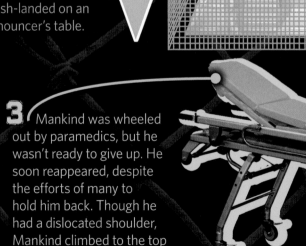

2 Mankind plummeted 16 feet (5 meters) and crash-landed on an announcer's table.

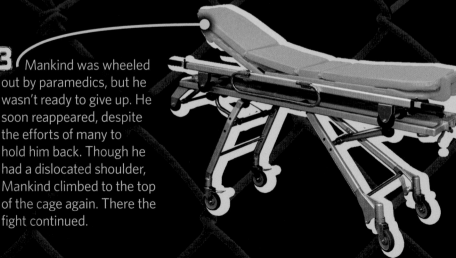

3 Mankind was wheeled out by paramedics, but he wasn't ready to give up. He soon reappeared, despite the efforts of many to hold him back. Though he had a dislocated shoulder, Mankind climbed to the top of the cage again. There the fight continued.

4 Back on top of the cage, Undertaker slammed Mankind down on his back. The force of the slam broke the cage ceiling. Again Mankind crashed to the ring floor. Undertaker jumped down after him.

5 Mankind was out cold for a couple minutes, but when he came to the fight continued. The men battled both in and out of the ring. At one point, Mankind threw a sack full of tacks on the mat.

6 After a vicious brawl, Undertaker pinned Mankind to the mat—on the pile of tacks.

CHAPTER 8
CHAMP STATUS

Undertaker's greatest claim to fame is his long history of *WrestleMania* wins. No other wrestler has even come close to matching Undertaker's record of 20 *WrestleMania* wins. But that's not his only notable achievement.

HEAVYWEIGHT WINS

Undertaker has taken more than his share of WWE World Heavyweight Championship titles. His first came at the November 1991 *Survivor Series*, a year after his debut. Undertaker defeated Hulk Hogan, but Hulk returned only six days later to recapture his title. Since then, Undertaker has gone on to win the big belt at least six times.

MAKING A RUMBLE

At the 2007 *Royal Rumble* on January 28, Undertaker drew number 30—making him the last wrestler to enter the ring. He eliminated everyone still standing, including his last opponent, Shawn Michaels. No one coming in at number 30 had ever won a Rumble match before.

UNDERTAKER'S WRESTLEMANIA "VICTIMS"

Year	Victim
1991	"Superfly" Jimmy Snuka
1992	Jake "the Snake" Roberts
1993	Giant Gonzalez
1995	King Kong Bundy
1996	Diesel
1997	Sycho Sid
1998	Kane
1999	Big Bossman
2001	Triple H
2002	Ric Flair
2003	Big Show and Albert
2004	Kane
2005	Randy Orton
2006	Mark Henry
2007	Batista
2008	Edge
2009	Shawn Michaels
2010	Shawn Michaels
2011	Triple H
2012	Triple H

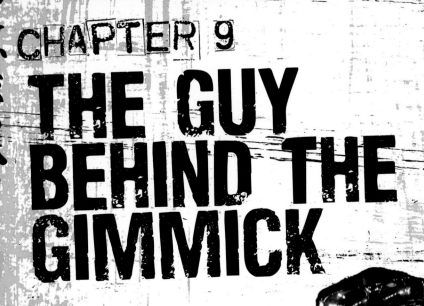

CHAPTER 9
THE GUY BEHIND THE GIMMICK

In the ring, Undertaker is mean and merciless. But there's another side to the man. That's the real-life Mark Calaway.

When it comes to his personal life, Mark keeps it separate from the hype of pro wrestling. So it's no wonder there are all kinds of false "facts" floating around about him. Check the sources and you'll find that even his name and birthday are subject to multiple versions. Here are a few facts you can rely on:

Real name: Mark William Calaway

Birthday: March 24, 1965

Born in: Houston, Texas

Sibling Status: youngest of five boys

ALL IN THE FAMILY

Mark married WWE **diva** Michelle McCool on June 26, 2010. He also has had two previous marriages. Mark fathered three children from those relationships. Gunner Vincent is his son with his first wife, Jodi Lynn. Daughters Chasey and Gracie were born while he was married to his second wife, Sara.

FACT

For the past few years, Mark has been working in real estate development. His firm is called Calahart Crossroads LLC.

diva—a female professional wrestler

CELEBRITY STATUS

Mark's Undertaker image has made him a pop culture icon. His star status has brought him even more fame through movies, music, merchandise, and more. Here are just a few examples.

MOVIES

Mark had a small part in the 1991 movie *Suburban Commando*. He played a bounty hunter.

COMICS

Undertaker has his own 10-part comic book series. There are also a few special editions that go along with the series.

POW!

CRUNCH!

DVDs

Undertaker's amazing career is documented in a long list of DVDs. Several of these DVDs even provide a rare interview clip or two.

TOYS

There are many different Undertaker action figures. There is an Undertaker teddy bear too. Burger King once offered a plush Taker toy in their kids' meals.

MUSIC

Undertaker was featured on an album in the 1990s called *WrestleMania: The Album*. His three-and-a-half minute instrumental theme song is called "The Man in Black."

UNDYING PHENOM

At *WrestleMania* 28 on April 1, 2012, Undertaker finished off Triple H to wrap up a 20-0 winning streak. With rumors swirling about retirement, what will Undertaker's next step be? Is the Phenom ready to leave the WWE limelight and enjoy life in a less brutal lane? Whether Undertaker chooses to retire or stay in the ring, he'll always be a legend in pro wrestling!

GLOSSARY

babyface (BAY-bee-fayss)—a wrestler who acts as a hero in the ring

biceps (BYE-seps)—the large muscle on the front of the arm between the shoulder and inner elbow

cult (KUHLT)—a strong, almost religious devotion to a person, a thing, an idea, or a way of life

debut (DAY-byoo)—a person's first public appearance

diva (DEE-vuh)—a female professional wrestler

feud (FYOOD)—a long-running quarrel between two people or groups of people

gimmick (GIM-ik)—a clever trick or idea used to get attention

hearse (HURSS)—a car that carries a coffin to a funeral and burial

heel (HEEL)—a wrestler who acts as a villain in the ring

mortician (mor-TISH-uhn)—a person who prepares dead bodies for funerals

orbital bone (OR-bih-tuhl BONE)—eye socket

stable (STAY-buhl)—a group of wrestlers who protect each other during matches and sometimes wrestle together

tag team (TAG TEEM)—when two wrestlers partner together against other teams

urn (URN)—a container that holds the ashes of a cremated body

READ MORE

Bringle, Jennifer. *Undertaker: Master of Pain.* Slam! Stars of Wrestling. New York: Rosen Pub., 2012.

O'Shei, Tim. *Undertaker.* Stars of Pro Wrestling. Mankato, Minn.: Capstone Press, 2010.

Sullivan, Kevin. *WWE Undertaker.* DK Readers. London; New York: DK Publishing, 2009.

INTERNET SITES

FactHound offers a safe, fun way to find Internet sites related to this book. All of the sites on FactHound have been researched by our staff.

Here's all you do:

Visit *www.facthound.com*

Enter this code: 9781429686792

INDEX